# Daddy's Deploying

## MARLENE NORGARD

ISBN 978-1-962729-01-7(Paperback)

Published in the United States by Inspire
An Adducent Creative Imprint
Adducent, Inc.
Jacksonville, Florida

To my son Deklan and my loving husband Patrick, your influence on my life has been tremendous. You've added color, troubles, zest, and meaning, our military journey has been full of highs and lows.

Throughout the deployments, training, lonely nights, and quiet households I have learned a great deal about my own strength as a mom, a wife, a cook, and a friend. It had been my pleasure to share all of our experiences together.

1

# Daddy's Deploying

My son, know I will always love you,
even when I leave.
When I'll be called to duty and we will be apart.
There will be miles between us,
But I will always love you from the bottom of
my heart.

The first few days I spend far from you
Will be the longest of them all
But look up in the sky, my son
And see the sun shining through

Know that when you look up there
That I will be looking too.
I will be missing your sweet smile
I will be thinking of only you.

Remember that you can always try to reach me
You can write a letter, or try and call
Sometimes it will be hard to hear me,
I may not answer,
But please keep on trying, through it all.

Know that I do the best I can
To keep you safe from harm,
It is my duty to my country
To protect it from any dark storm.

So when you lie in bed at night
And are scared of creatures lurking
Know I am protecting you my son,
And I am up for hours working.

I know that you will miss my hugs
And that you will want to tell me stories
Of all the adventures that you've had
And all of your daily worries

Know that you can still talk to mommy
Know that I will be there too
Look up at the sky, the sun, the moon
I will always be here for you.

Keep a journal of your tales,
Write when you are blue
Try and read it out loud to me,
I will try my best to answer you.

Daddy has very important work to do
But I always take time to think of you
Each day I think of a memory together
I hope you remember the good times too.

So when you are feeling lonely just remember,
My son, I'll love you from sea to sea
In my life you'll always be first
You will always have a place right next to me.

22

# ABOUT THE AUTHOR

Born and raised in New Jersey in a small country town full of horses, farms, wide open fields, and mountains as our backdrop, I never imagined how much bigger my world would become.

I got my Bachelor's Degree in Criminal Justice and Associate of Science Degree in Crime Scene Technology and worked as a crime scene technician. I married the love of my life as he entered the US Marine Corps. Now, I'm a military spouse and a mother of two beautiful children. And I found my niche in writing.

Experiencing the many outlooks, chal-lenges, and hardships of military life and seeing not only my chil-dren but also my friends' children struggle with specific issues within that life, I have made it my mission to write about those issues and open a dialogue for conversations about them. I am the author of the children's books *Daddy's Deploying, Kali's Travels,* and *My Star-Spangled Friend*. This series means a lot to me. I thank my son Deklan and daughter Kali for their compassion and understanding. They entrusted me with their feelings I could use to write these books that I hope will help connect you with your child to show them that others feel just the same. It's okay to feel as they do and to know we can do something about it. We can talk, share, and make sure they feel safe and loved wherever they are.

www.MarlenesMilitaryKids.com